For our dear Abby

Happy Easter

from G.G.

March 30, 1997

Text & Design by Anne McRae
Illustrated by Fiammetta Dogi
This edition edited by Nina Rosenstein

Created and produced by McRae Books
Borgo Ognissanti, 62 - Florence, Italy

Printed in Italy
ISBN 0-517-12432-7

My First

Picture Dictionary

Illustrated by Fiammetta Dogi
with Susanna Addario, Matteo Chesi,
Claudia Saraceni, Roberto Simoni

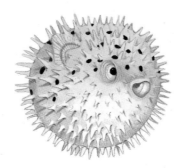

DERRYDALE BOOKS
New York • Avenel

Our Bodies

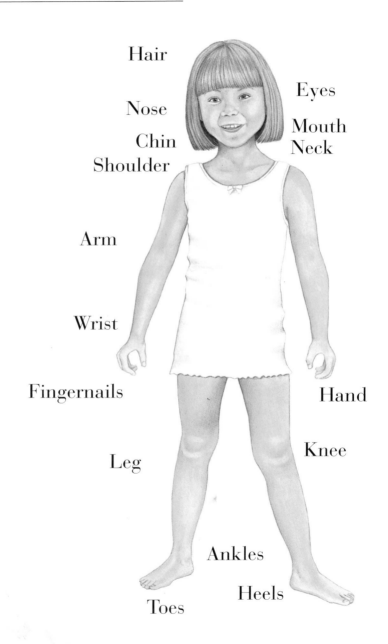

Hair

Eyes

Nose

Mouth
Neck

Chin

Shoulder

Arm

Wrist

Fingernails

Hand

Knee

Leg

Ankles

Heels

Toes

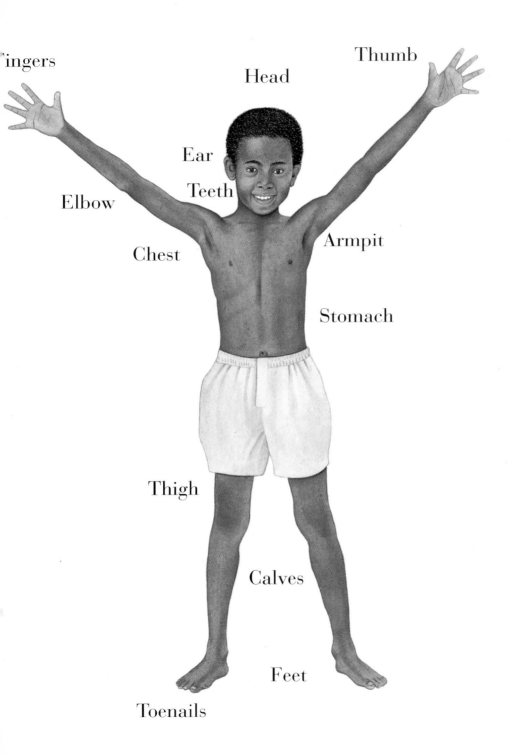

Fingers

Head

Thumb

Ear

Teeth

Elbow

Armpit

Chest

Stomach

Thigh

Calves

Feet

Toenails

Grandma's Birthday

Daddy

Mommy

Grandpa

Baby brother

Me

Grandma

Birthday cake

Aunt

Uncle

Cousin

Sister

Teddy

Presents

My House

Second floor

Window

Front door

Shingles

Ground floor

Garage

Mailbox

Hedge

Automatic door

Steps

Driveway

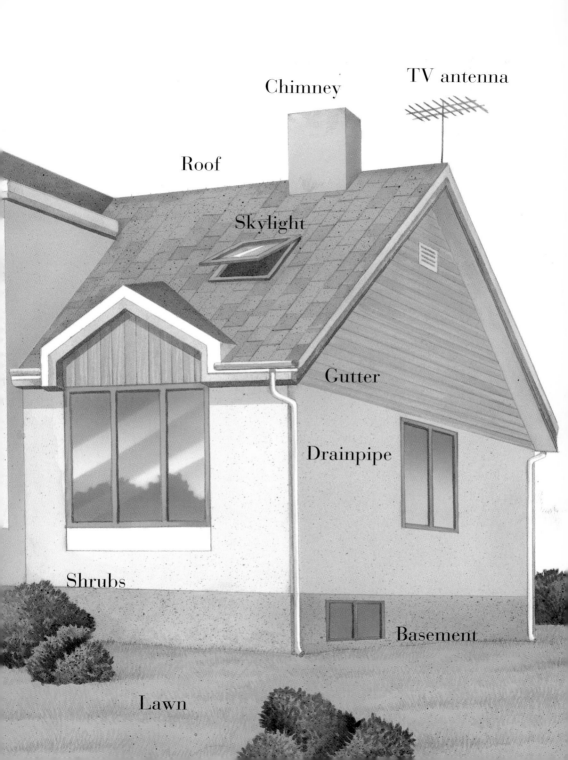

Chimney

TV antenna

Roof

Skylight

Gutter

Drainpipe

Shrubs

Basement

Lawn

My Room

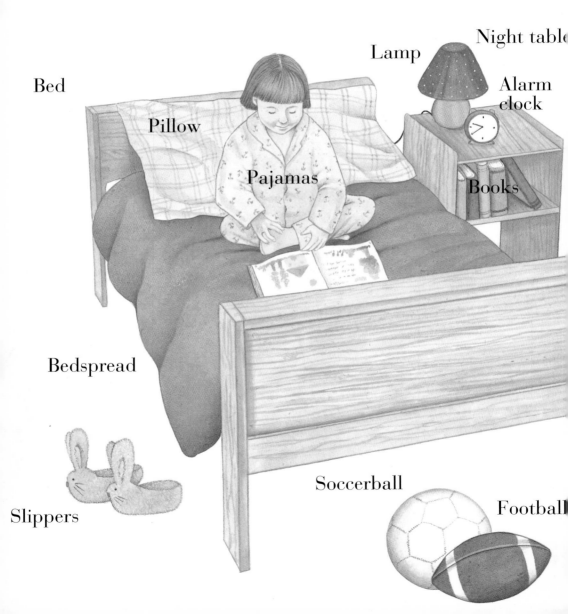

Night table

Lamp

Bed

Alarm clock

Pillow

Pajamas

Books

Bedspread

Soccerball

Slippers

Football

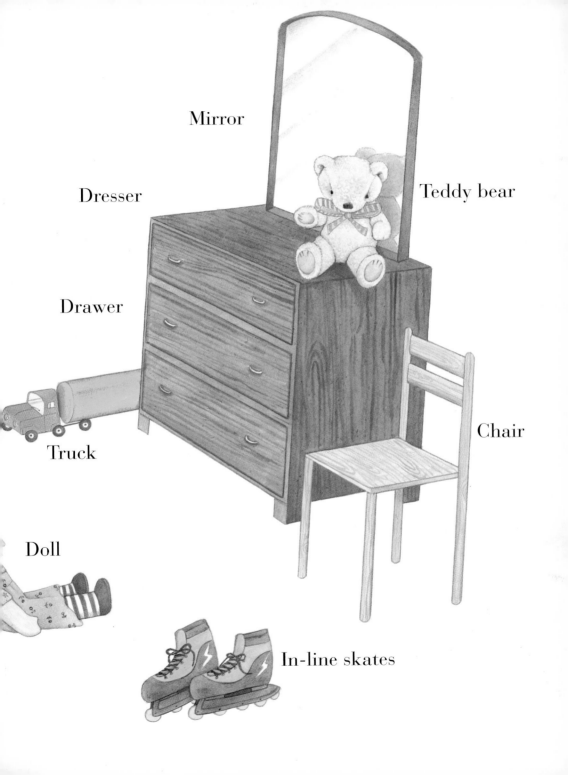

Mirror

Dresser

Teddy bear

Drawer

Truck

Chair

Doll

In-line skates

My Favorite Clothes

Sweater

Jacket

Book
bag

T-shirt

Shorts

Laces

Sneakers

Cap

Blouse

Hood

Sweater

Sweatshirt

Skirt

Sandals

Sweat pants

Socks

Shoes

School Days

Clock

Bulletin board

Alphabet

ABCDEF

Cabinets

Globe

Desk

Rug

Computer

Screen

Chair

Keyboard

Mouse

Map

Calendar

Blackboard

Teacher

Painting

cher's
esk

Student

Brushes

Easel

Paints

Pen

Books

Pencil

ckpack

Glue

Crayons

Scissors

Notebook

At the Beach

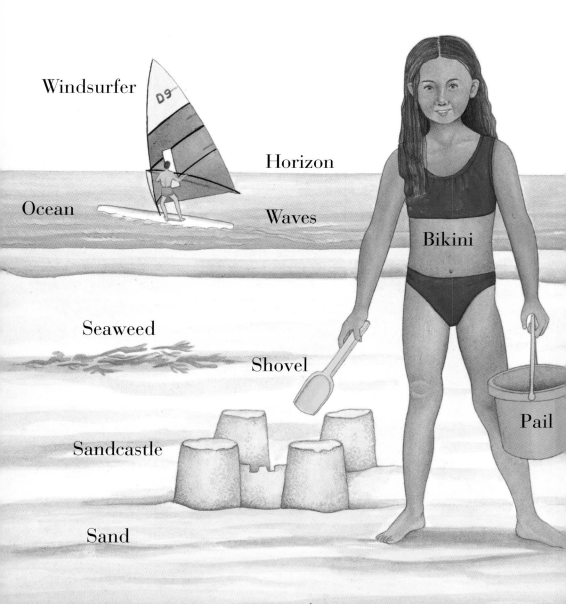

Windsurfer

Horizon

Ocean

Waves

Bikini

Seaweed

Shovel

Sandcastle

Pail

Sand

Seagulls

Sailboat

Sun hat

Beach umbrella

Sunglasses

Swim suit

Swim trunks

Suntan lotion

Beach towel

Swim tube

Crab

Shells

In the Mountains

Snowman

Hat

Warm jacket

Earmuffs

Scarf

Carrot nose

Snowball

Buttons

Mukluks

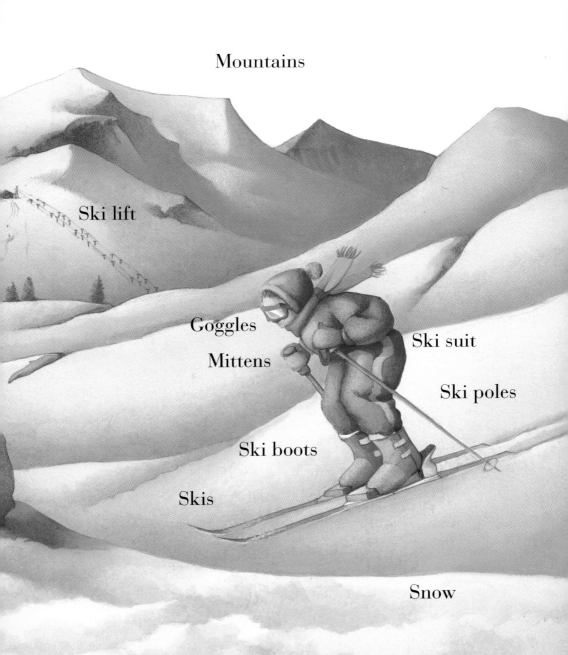

Mountains

Ski lift

Goggles

Mittens

Ski suit

Ski poles

Ski boots

Skis

Snow

We've Been Shopping

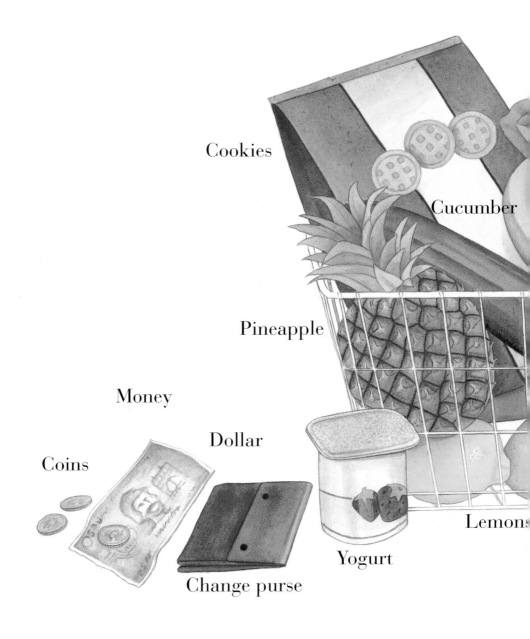

Cookies

Cucumber

Pineapple

Money

Dollar

Coins

Yogurt

Lemons

Change purse

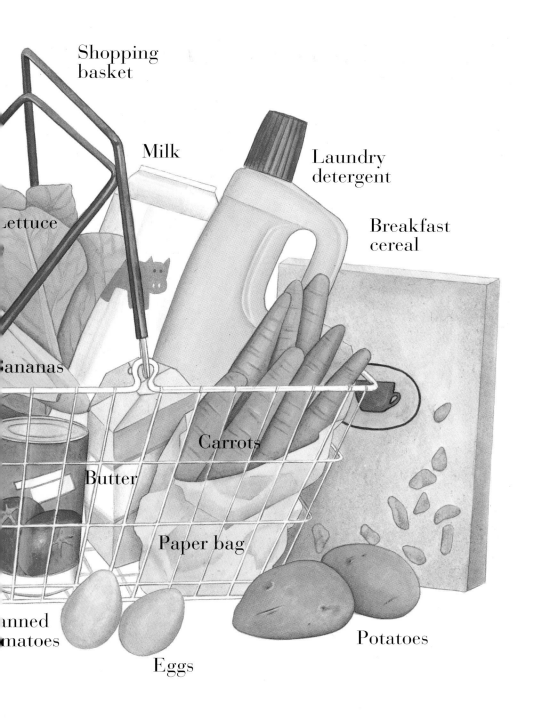

Shopping basket

Milk

Laundry detergent

Breakfast cereal

Lettuce

Bananas

Carrots

Butter

Paper bag

Canned tomatoes

Eggs

Potatoes

Dinnertime

Soup spoon

Tomato soup

Salad

Wa pit

Rolls

Knife

Plate

Glass

Napkin

Salt

Pepper

F

Tablecloth

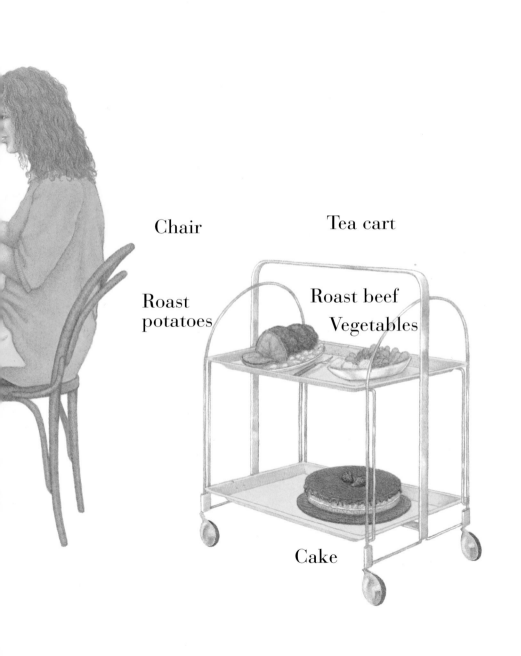

Chair

Tea cart

Roast
potatoes

Roast beef
Vegetables

Cake

At the Circus

Tightrope

Acrobat

Lion

Juggler

Ball

Unicycle

Circus horse

Seal

Arena

Hoop

Whip

Trapeze

Spotlight

Trapeze
artist

Ladder

Lion
tamer

Clown

Platform

The Vegetable Garden

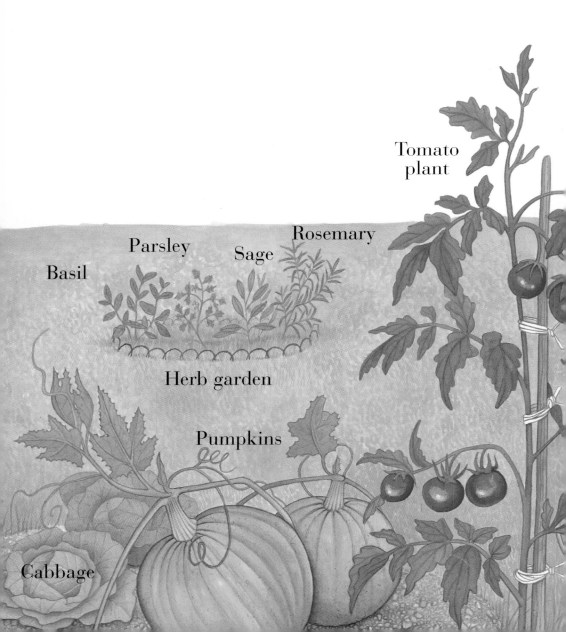

Tomato
plant

Rosemary

Parsley

Sage

Basil

Herb garden

Pumpkins

Cabbage

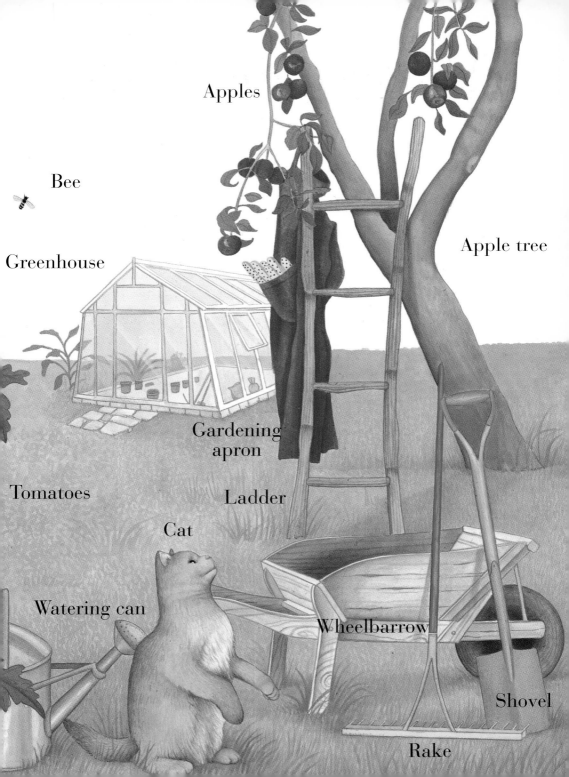

Apples

Bee

Greenhouse

Apple tree

Gardening
apron

Tomatoes

Ladder

Cat

Watering can

Wheelbarrow

Shovel

Rake

Down on the Farm

Cow

Pasture

Calf

Gate

Fence

Rooster

Hen

Chickens

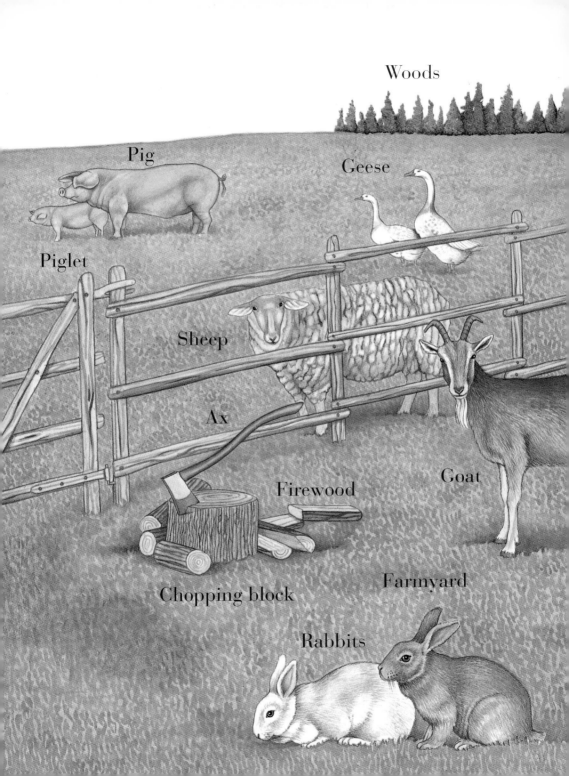

Woods

Pig

Geese

Piglet

Sheep

Ax

Goat

Firewood

Chopping block

Farmyard

Rabbits

At the Zoo

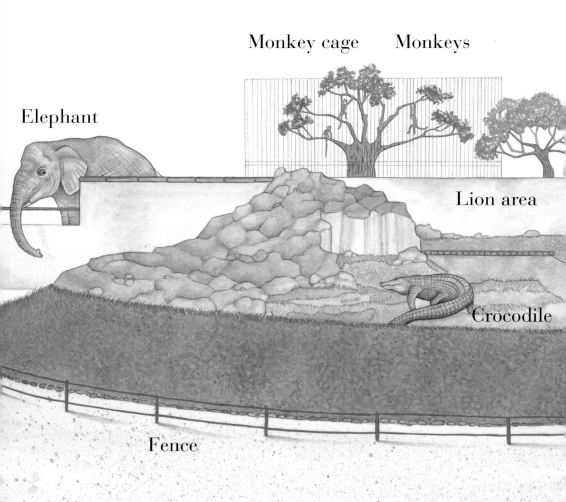

Monkey cage   Monkeys

Elephant

Lion area

Crocodile

Fence

Aviary

Birds

Entrance

Animal
house

Ticket office

Lion

Wall

Sign

Visitors

Camping Out

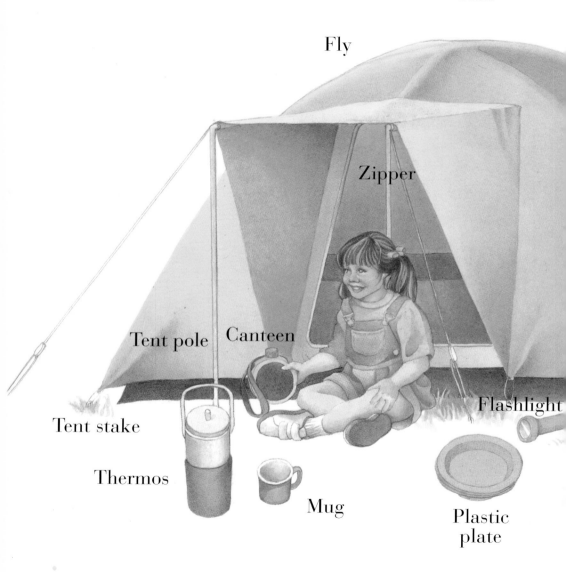

Tent

Fly

Zipper

Canteen

Tent pole

Tent stake

Thermos

Mug

Flashlight

Plastic
plate

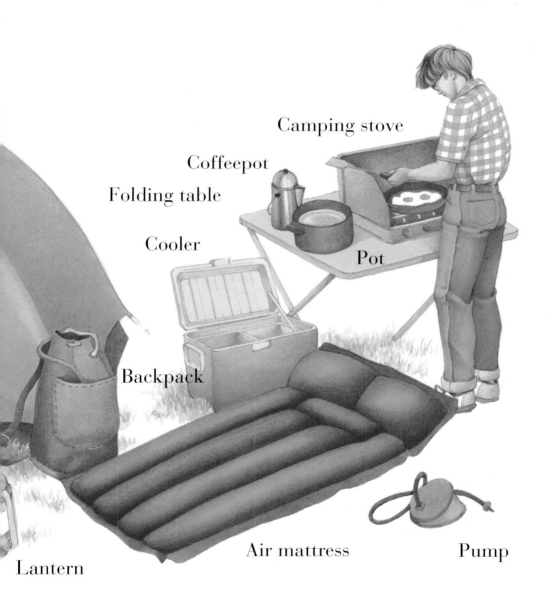

Camping stove

Coffeepot

Folding table

Cooler

Pot

Backpack

Lantern

Air mattress

Pump

In the Park

Tree

Bird's nest

Leaves

Squirrel

Swings

Children

Park bench

Trash can

Handbag

Dog

Stick

Kite

Houses

Jogger

Helmet

Brook

Bridge

Cyclist

Grass

Mountain
bike

Path

A Tropical Forest

Flowers

Insect

Stem

Leaves

Fern

Toucan

Roots

Leopard

Plant

Tree trunk

Bar

Spider

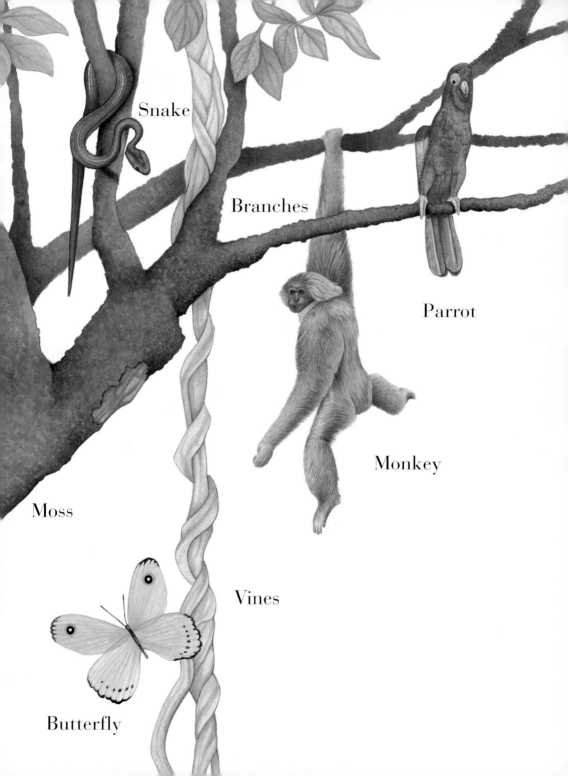

Snake

Branches

Parrot

Monkey

Moss

Vines

Butterfly

Snorkeling

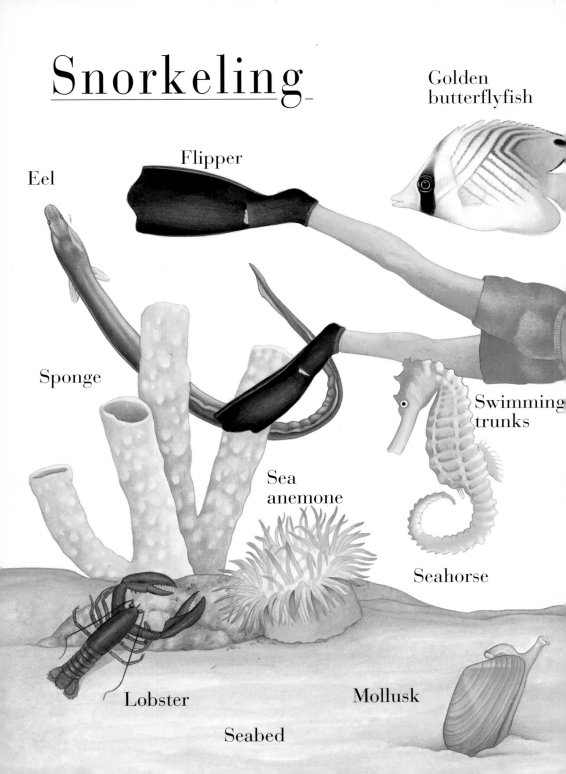

Golden
butterflyfish

Flipper

Eel

Sponge

Swimming
trunks

Sea
anemone

Seahorse

Lobster

Mollusk

Seabed

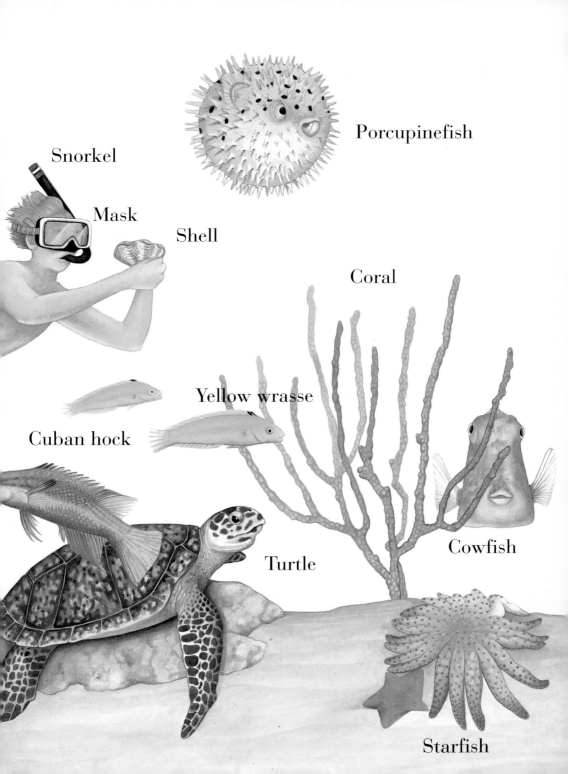

Porcupinefish

Snorkel

Mask

Shell

Coral

Yellow wrasse

Cuban hock

Cowfish

Turtle

Starfish

Our World

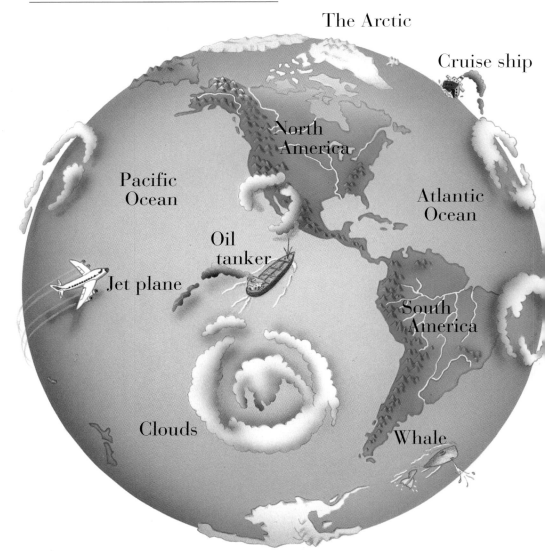

The Arctic

Cruise ship

North
America

Pacific
Ocean

Atlantic
Ocean

Oil
tanker

Jet plane

South
America

Clouds

Whale

South Pole

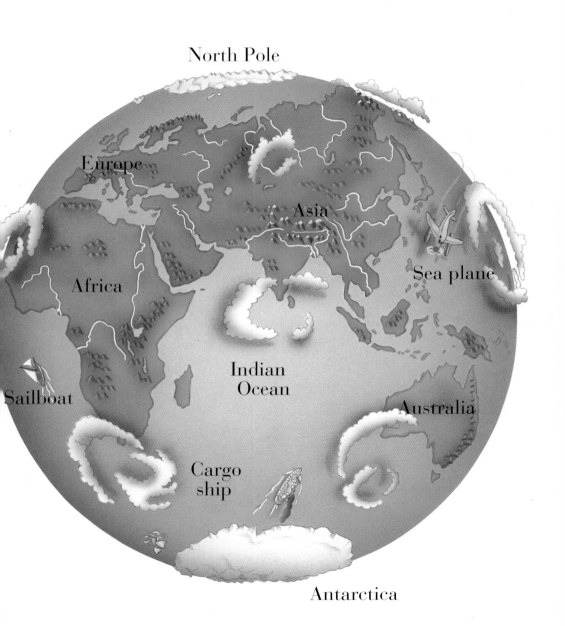

Our Solar System

Saturn

Rings

Uranus

Outer
space

Neptune

Pluto

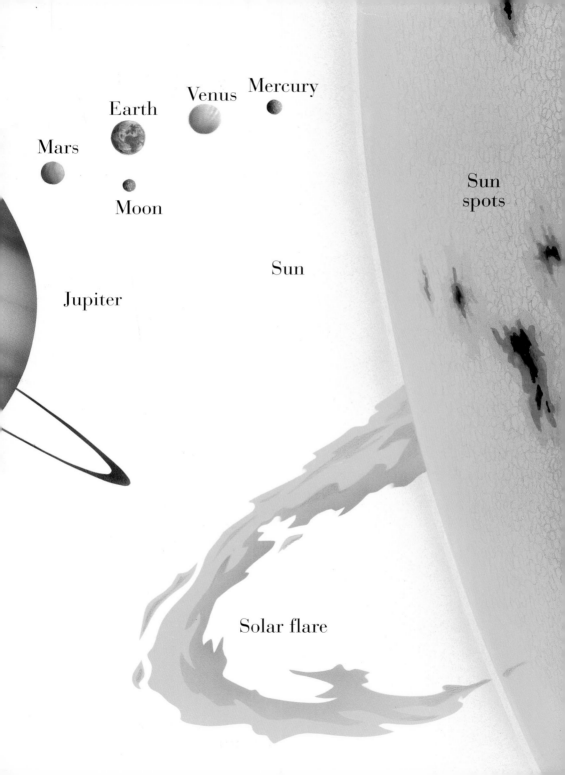

Mercury

Venus

Earth

Mars

Moon

Jupiter

Sun

Sun
spots

Solar flare